DISNEY·PIXAR
BRAVE

Learn to draw Merida,
Elinor, Angus, and other characters
from Disney/Pixar's *Brave*
step by step!

Illustrated by The Disney Storybook Artists

Walter Foster Jr.

This library edition published in 2015 by Walter Foster Jr.,
an imprint of Quarto Publishing Group USA Inc.
3 Wrigley, Suite A
Irvine, CA 92618

Distributed in the United States and Canada by
Lerner Publisher Services
241 First Avenue North
Minneapolis, MN 55401 U.S.A.
www.lernerbooks.com

First Library Edition

Library of Congress Cataloging-in-Publication Data

Learn to draw Disney/Pixar Brave (Walter Foster (Firm))
  Learn to draw Disney/Pixar Brave / illustrated by The Disney Storybook Artists. -- First Library
Edition.
    pages cm
  "Learn to draw Merida, Elinor, Angus, and other characters from Disney/Pixar's Brave step by
step!"
  ISBN 978-1-939581-45-7
1. Fantasy in art--Juvenile literature. 2. Heroines in art--Juvenile literature. 3. Drawing--Technique-
-Juvenile literature. 4. Brave (Motion picture)--Juvenile literature. I. Disney Storybook Artists,
illustrator. II. Title.
  NC1764.8.F37L43 2015
  741.5'1--dc23
                                                                                          2014017649

062015
18882

9 8 7 6 5 4 3 2 1

TABLE OF CONTENTS

❄ THE STORY OF BRAVE ❄

Merida is the adventurous Princess of DunBroch, who is more comfortable shooting her bow than wearing ball gowns. Independent and feisty, Merida is horrified that her parents have invited the lords of three neighboring clans to bring their sons to the castle for a competition—where the prize is Merida's hand in marriage!

Determined to avoid the fate that awaits her, Merida defies this age-old tradition and instead participates in the archery competition to win her own hand in marriage. She shoots all three bullseyes to win the competition, but her defiance causes a ruckus in the kingdom and an argument with her mother. Merida runs away and rides into the forest on her horse, Angus. She soon comes across a witch who gives her a spell cake that, Merida hopes, will change her mother's mind about the princess's marriage.

As soon as Elinor eats the cake, she is transformed into a bear. As Merida and Elinor fight to transform Elinor back into the queen she is, they embark on a journey of bravery to prove that love can beat all odds.

TOOLS AND MATERIALS

Before you begin, gather some drawing tools, such as paper,
a regular pencil, an eraser, and a pencil sharpener. For color, you can use
markers, colored pencils, crayons, or even paint!

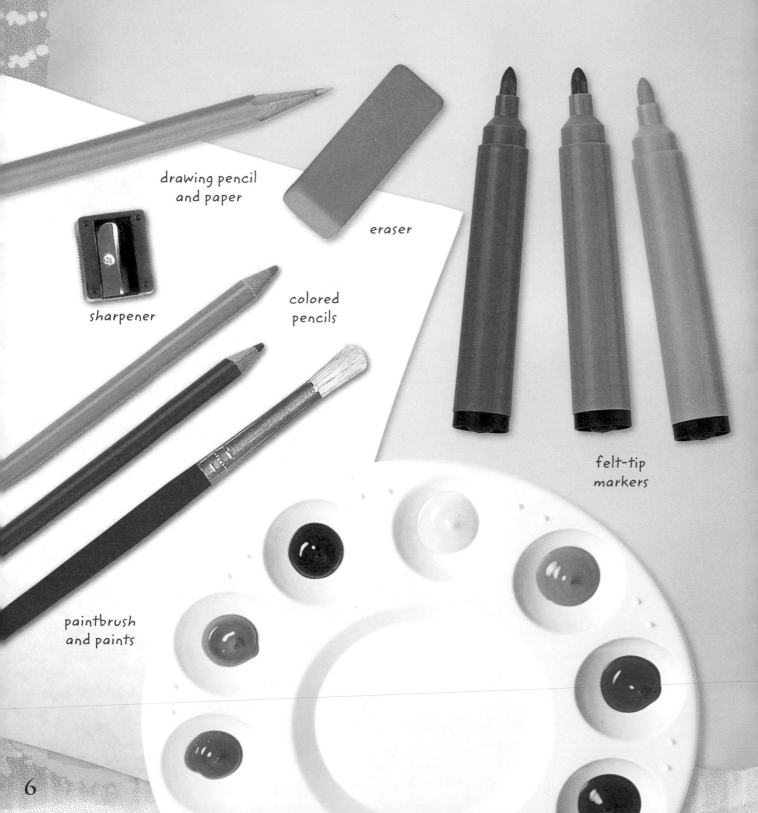

drawing pencil
and paper

eraser

sharpener

colored
pencils

felt-tip
markers

paintbrush
and paints

HOW TO USE THIS BOOK

Follow the steps like the ones shown below, and you will be drawing Merida, the triplet cubs, and the other characters from *Brave* in no time!

First draw basic shapes using light lines that will be easy to erase.

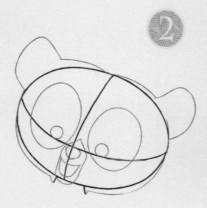

Each new step is shown in blue, so you'll know what to add next.

Follow the blue lines to draw the details.

Now darken the lines you want to keep, and erase the rest.

Use some magic (or crayons or markers) to add color to your drawing!

DRAWING EXERCISES

Warm up your hand by drawing squiggles and shapes on a piece of scrap paper.

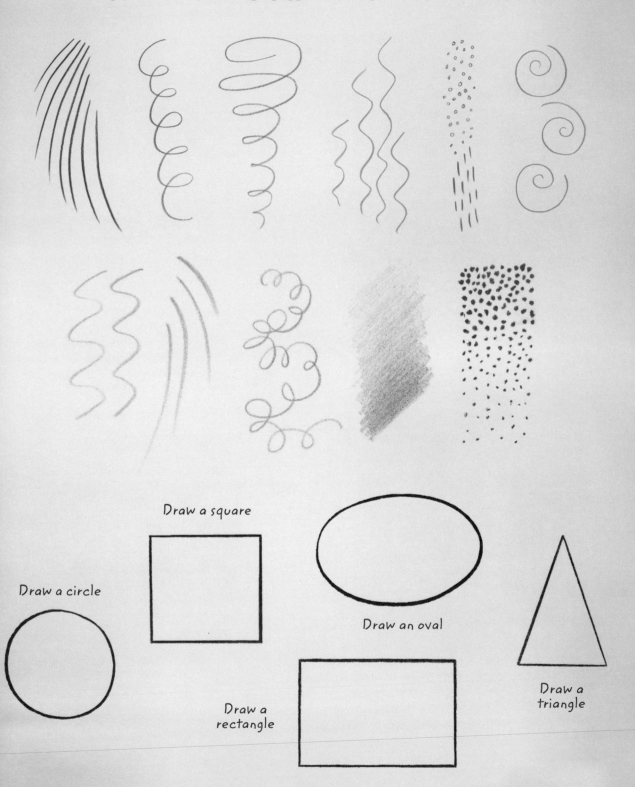

Draw a square

Draw a circle

Draw an oval

Draw a rectangle

Draw a triangle

If you can draw a few basic shapes, you can draw just about anything!

Circle   Carriage   Rectangle   Book

Triangle   Palace   Oval   Teapot   Square   Clock tower

Look how you can turn your doodles into drawings!

Butterfly   Tiara   Balloon

Gown   Bird

MERIDA

Merida is the adventurous Princess of DunBroch. More comfortable in the woods with her bow than in a ball gown, Merida would be perfectly content to ride her horse, Angus, around all day in the sunshine.

for Merida's
hair, use wild,
squiggly lines

Merida's eyes

NO!   YES!

MERIDA IN ACTION

Fergus and Elinor invited the lords of the Highland clans to present their sons as suitors in a
competition to win Merida's hand in marriage. To avoid marrying one of the lords' sons, Merida
shocks everyone by competing for her own hand in the archery competition. She hits each bullseye to
win the competition, but in the process she causes a ruckus in the kingdom.

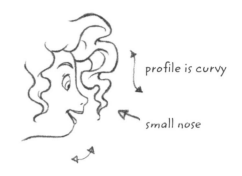

profile is curvy

small nose

ANGUS

Angus is Merida's trusty Clydesdale horse. Though he doesn't talk, he seems to understand Merida better than anyone else, and he plays with her and comforts her whenever she needs it.

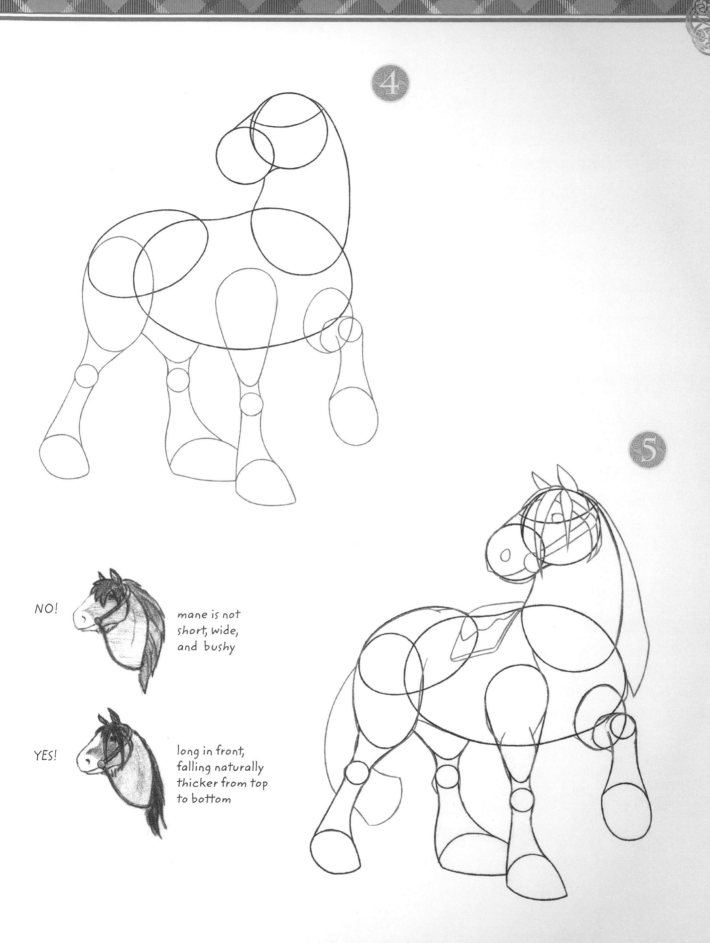

④

⑤

NO!

mane is not short, wide, and bushy

YES!

long in front, falling naturally thicker from top to bottom

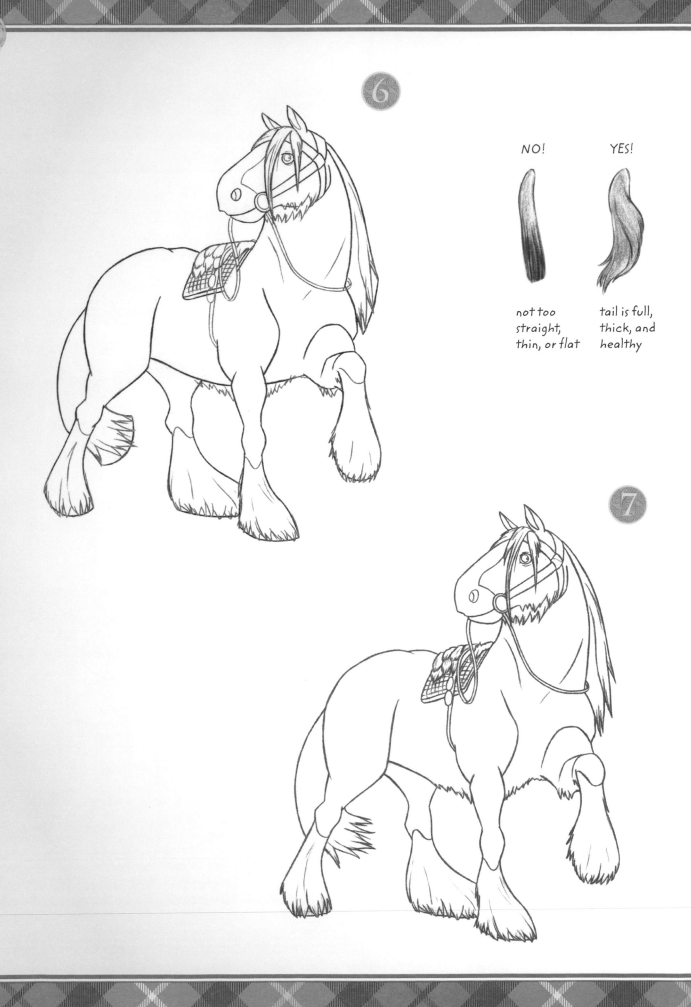

6

NO!   YES!

not too
straight,
thin, or flat

tail is full,
thick, and
healthy

7

NO!　YES!

not bare　covered
by hair

QUEEN ELINOR

As Queen of DunBroch, Elinor relies on tradition and diplomacy to rule the kingdom. Though she carries a lot of responsibility, there is a strong spirit inside Elinor that allows her to eventually connect with her audacious daughter, Merida.

④

NO!   no individual lashes

YES!   eye is almond shaped, with one line for eyelashes

⑤

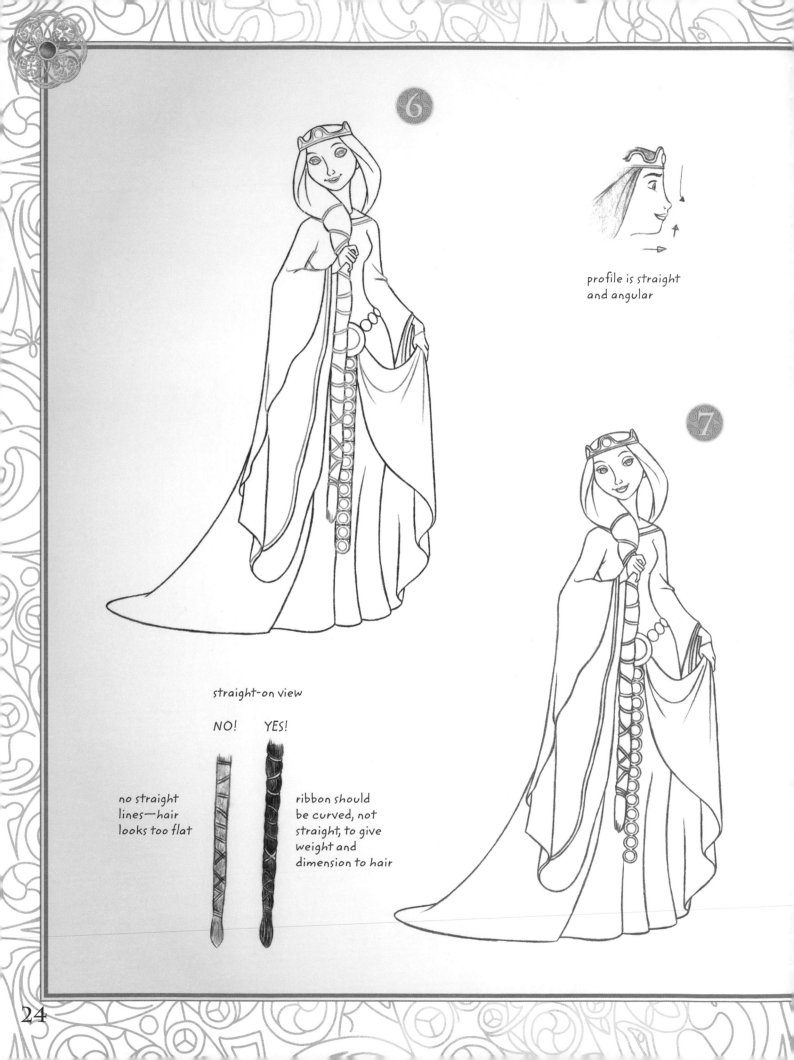

profile is straight
and angular

straight-on view

NO!   YES!

no straight
lines—hair
looks too flat

ribbon should
be curved, not
straight, to give
weight and
dimension to hair

24

side view
close up

hair is straight
and heavy in a
long ponytail

KING FERGUS

An adventurer at heart, Fergus is always eager to teach his daughter, Merida, a thing or two on the bow and sword. Years ago, to save Elinor and Merida, Fergus fought the vicious bear Mor'du and lost his leg, but that hasn't dampened his jovial nature.

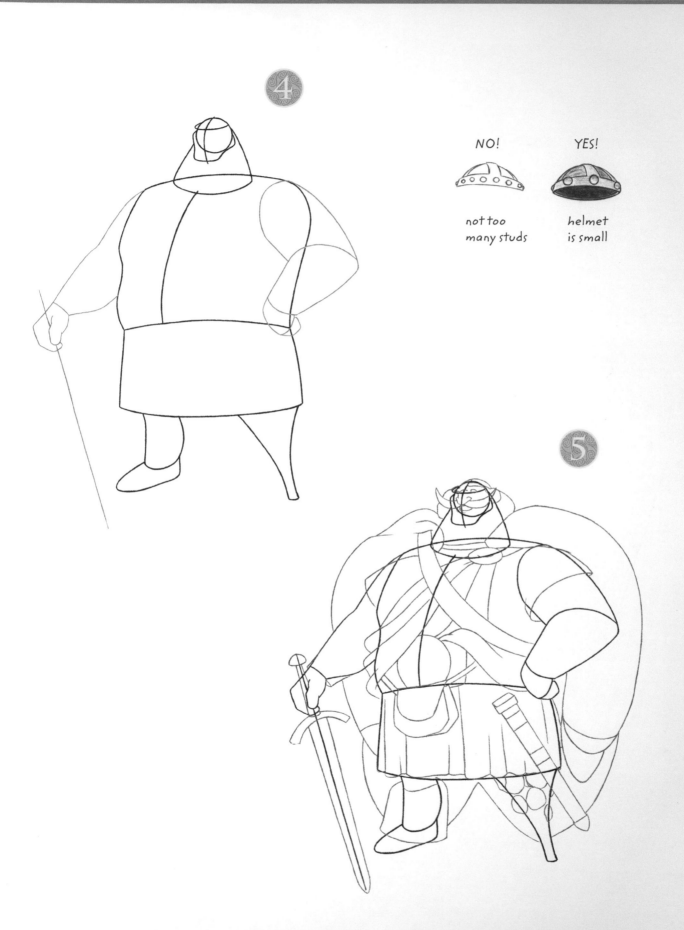

4

NO!

YES!

not too
many studs

helmet
is small

5

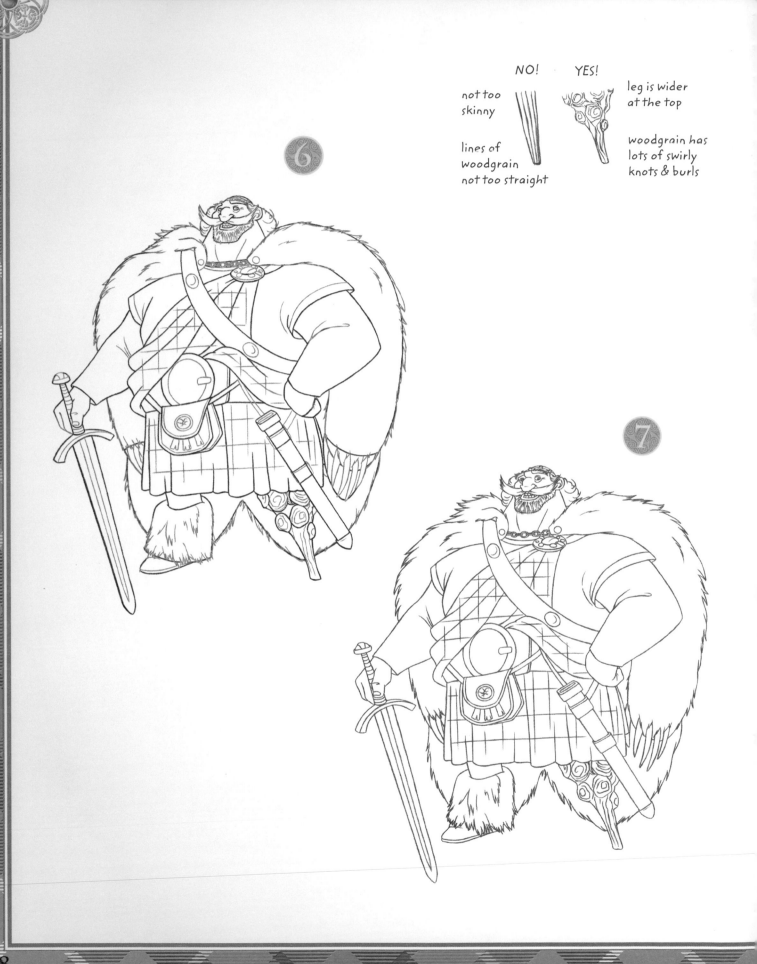

NO!   YES!

not too
skinny

lines of
woodgrain
not too straight

leg is wider
at the top

woodgrain has
lots of swirly
knots & burls

6

7

ELINOR THE BEAR

Elinor is transformed into a bear when she eats a cake that the Witch gave to Merida.
Merida and Elinor the Bear embark on a journey to find the Witch to change Elinor back,
and in the process, mother and daughter grow closer than ever.

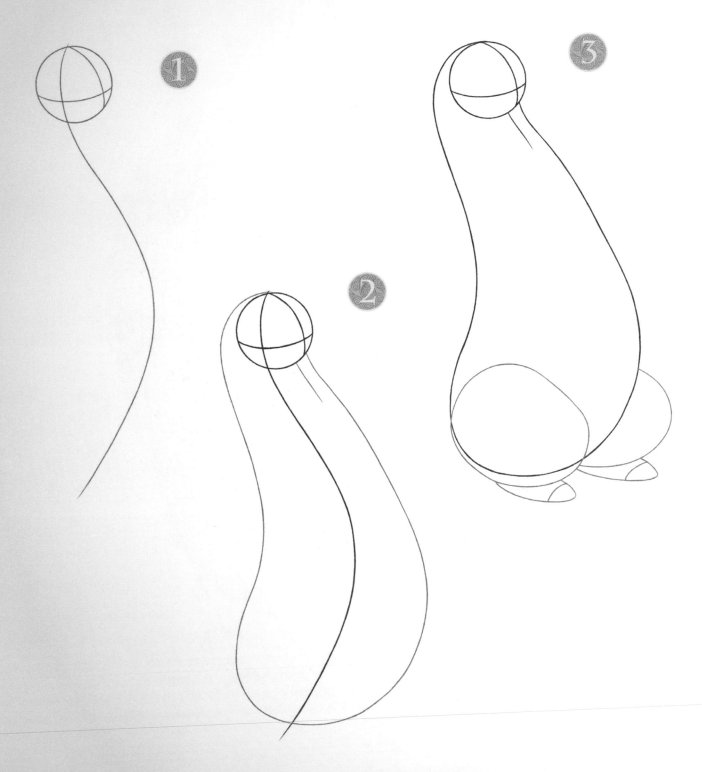

NO!

not spaced
too evenly

YES!

five claws
grouped
together

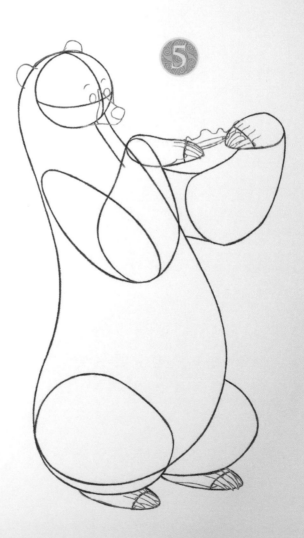

6

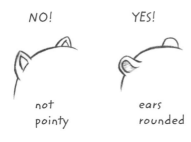

NO!   YES!

not
pointy

ears
rounded

no cartoony eyes

7

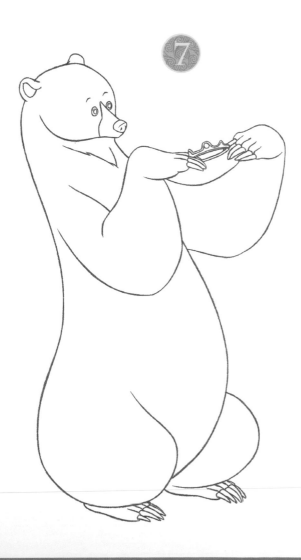

ELINOR THE BEAR IN ACTION

Elinor the Bear isn't sure what to eat one morning, so Merida teaches her how to fish like a real bear.
Reluctant at first, Elinor the Bear finally joins in and plays in the stream with Merida.

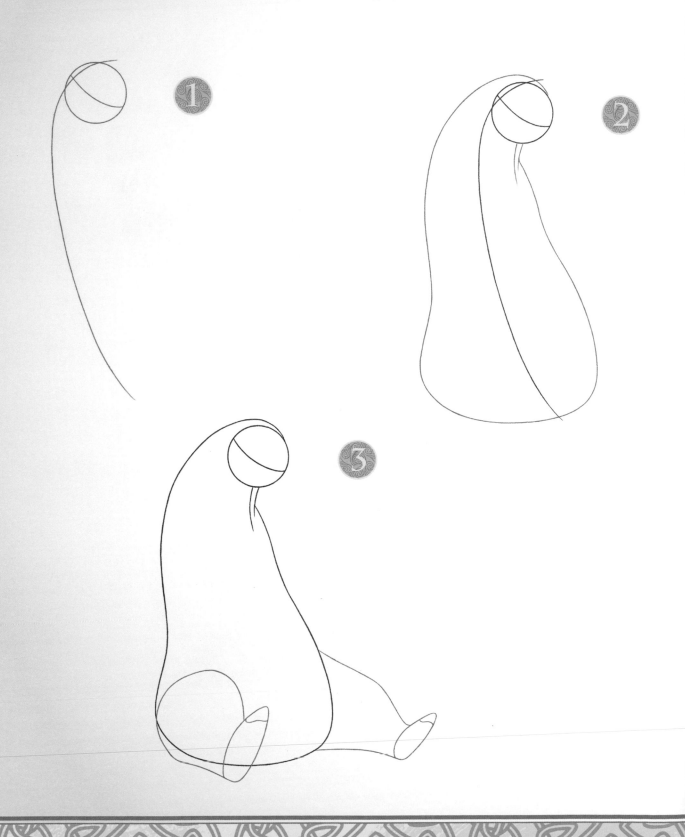

④

NO!   YES!

not too fuzzy   fur is smooth

⑤

NO!

not too big
and round

YES!

nose & eyes
proportioned

MOR'DU IN ACTION

Mor'du is the monstrous bear that interrupted a royal family picnic when Merida was just a wee lass. Years later, Merida and Elinor discover that Mor'du is actually a cursed ancient prince.

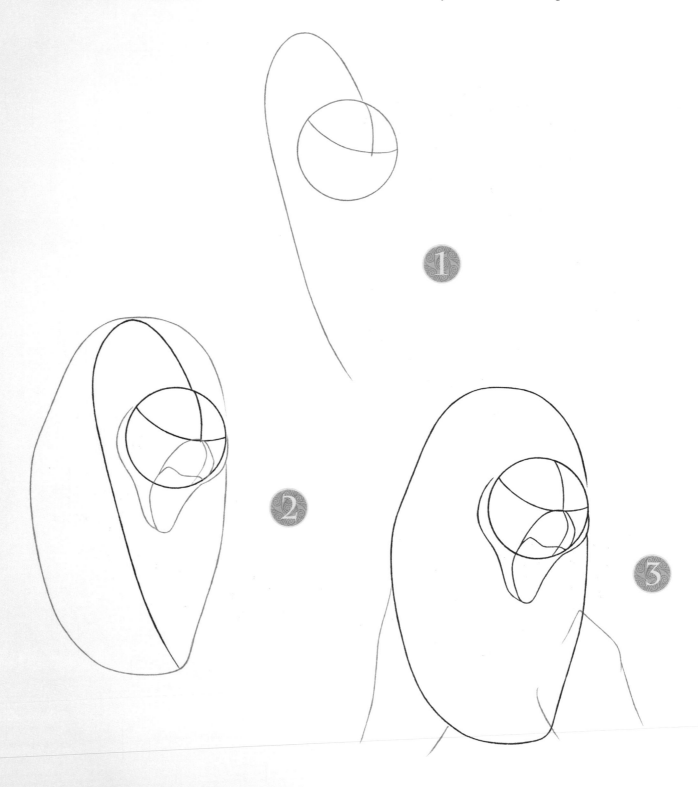

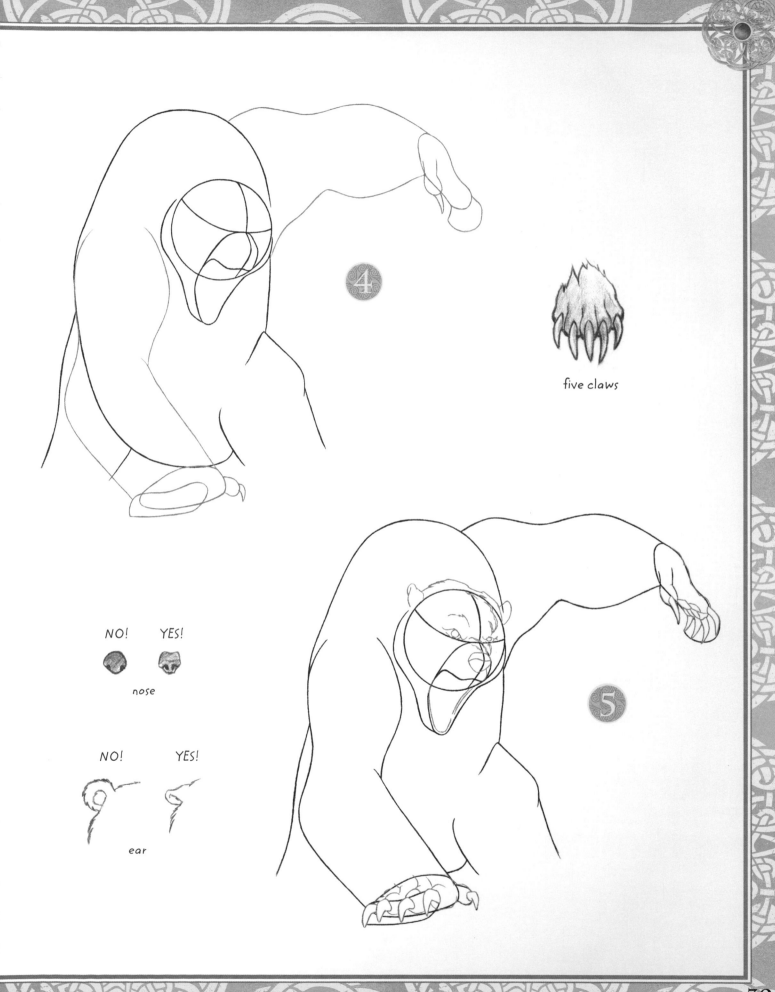

five claws

NO! YES!

nose

NO! YES!

ear

bald patches
and many scars

scars on
Mor'du's
nose

left eye
is blind
(white) and
has a scar

broken spears
and arrows on
his back

hump on neck
has no fur

fur is matted,
not smooth

THE WITCH

Because she is a reluctant witch, the Witch disguises herself as a wood-carver.
In Merida's desperate attempt to fix things with her mother, Merida finally convinces
the reluctant Witch to make a spell cake to give her mother, in hopes that it will make
Elinor change her mind about Merida's betrothal.

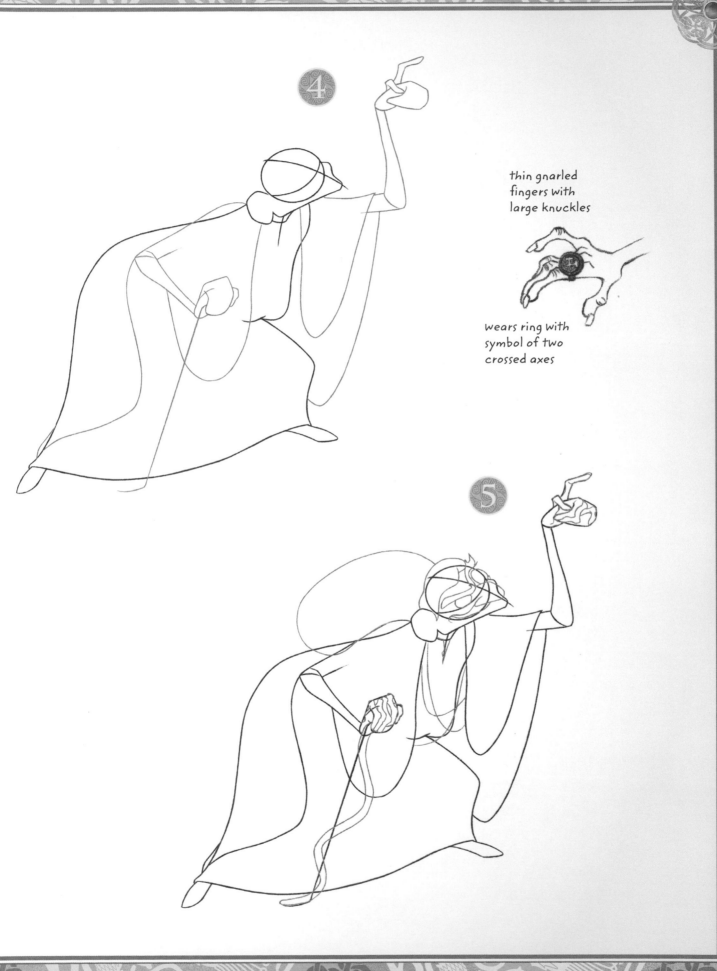

thin gnarled
fingers with
large knuckles

wears ring with
symbol of two
crossed axes

④

⑤

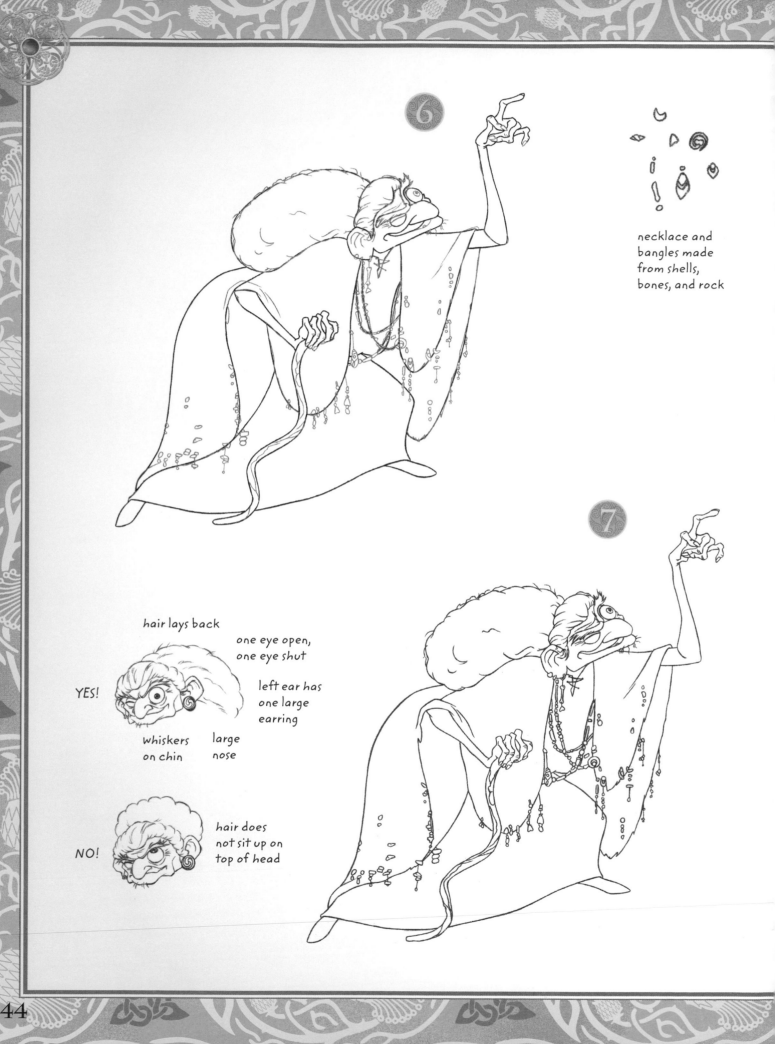

necklace and
bangles made
from shells,
bones, and rock

hair lays back

one eye open,
one eye shut

left ear has
one large
earring

whiskers
on chin

large
nose

YES!

NO!

hair does
not sit up on
top of head

companion is a
black raven

YES!   NO!

right ear
is large with
earrings

not small
or pointy

THE TRIPLETS

Harris, Hubert, and Hamish are Merida's identical-triplet brothers. Though they are troublemakers, they adore Merida and would do anything for her.

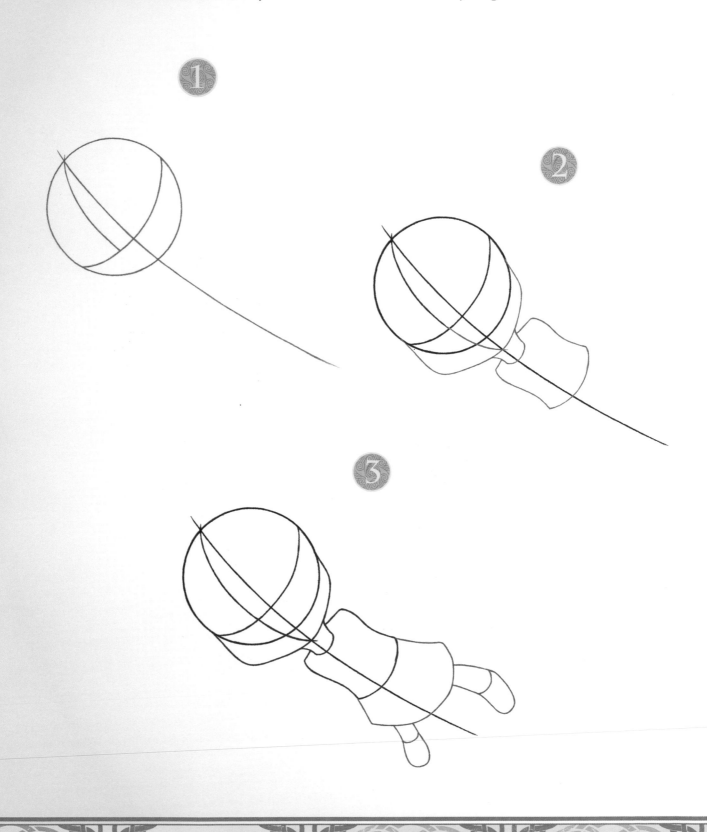

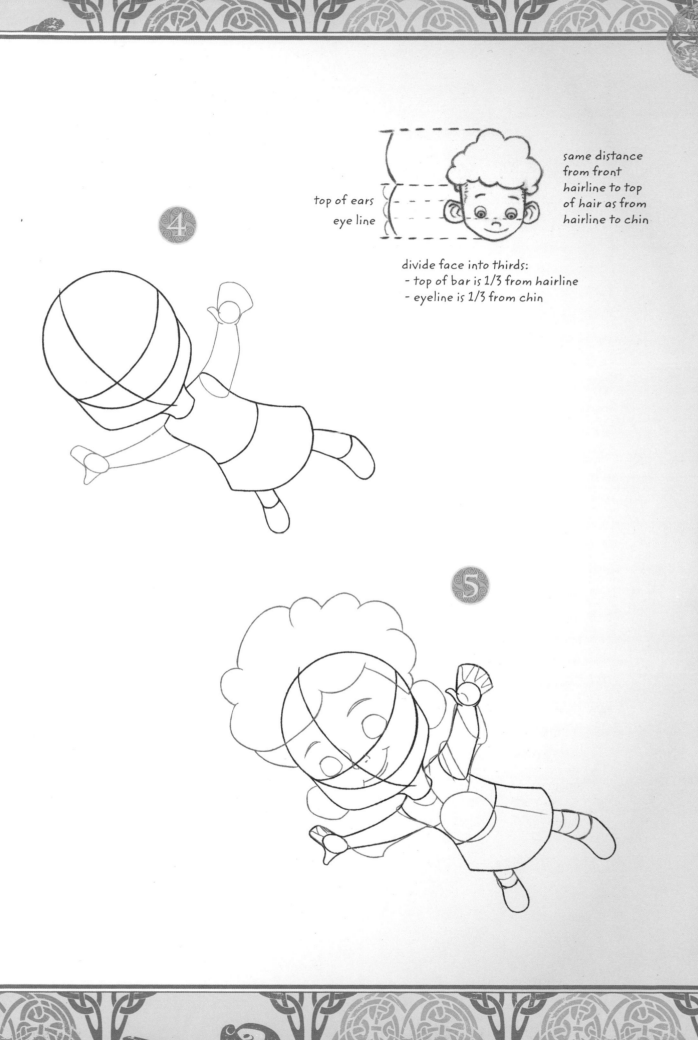

same distance
from front
hairline to top
of hair as from
hairline to chin

top of ears
eye line

divide face into thirds:
- top of bar is 1/3 from hairline
- eyeline is 1/3 from chin

a few
loose hairs

curly hair
on top,
cut short
on the
sides

NO!

pupils and
eyes not
too large

THE TRIPLET CUBS

Harris, Hubert, and Hamish eat some of the cake that Merida brought back from the Witch, so they all turn into bears just like their mother. Even though they're bear cubs, they still know when Merida's in trouble, and they love to come to her rescue.

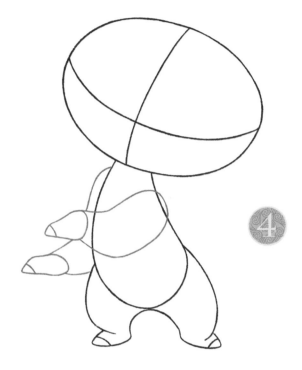

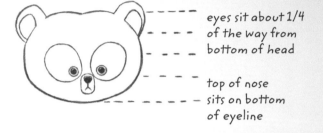

eyes sit about 1/4
of the way from
bottom of head

top of nose
sits on bottom
of eyeline

④

NO!

YES!

eyes cannot
move like this

eyes set close
together

⑤

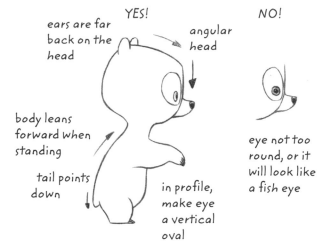

ears are far back on the head

body leans forward when standing

tail points down

YES!

angular head

in profile, make eye a vertical oval

NO!

eye not too round, or it will look like a fish eye

6

YES!   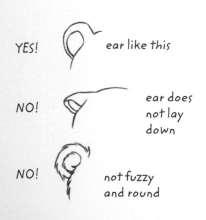   ear like this

NO!   ear does not lay down

NO!   not fuzzy and round

7

THE SONS OF LORDS MACGUFFIN, MACINTOSH, AND DINGWALL

Lords MacGuffin, MacIntosh, and Dingwall are the three lords of the Highland kingdom, and they haven't always gotten along. Even in this time of peace, they don't hesitate to let their sons—Young MacGuffin, Young MacIntosh, and Wee Dingwall—compete against each other for Merida's hand in marriage.

head is jelly bean shaped

5

6

7

Young
MacIntosh

Lord
MacIntosh

NO!

YES!

hair not
too big and
poofy

hair is
wavy, curly,
and large

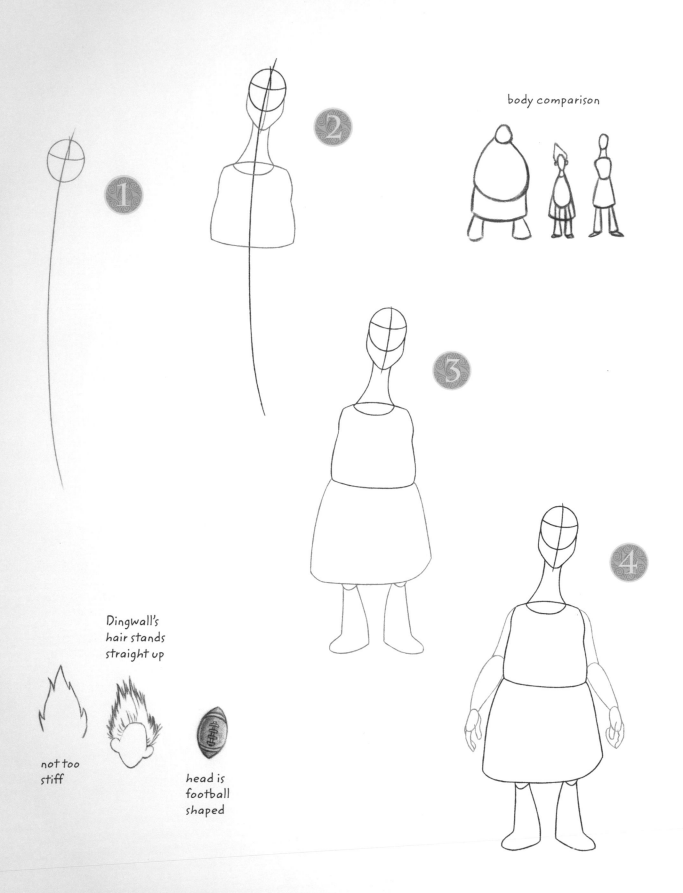

body comparison

Dingwall's
hair stands
straight up

not too
stiff

head is
football
shaped

Wee
Dingwall

Lord
Dingwall

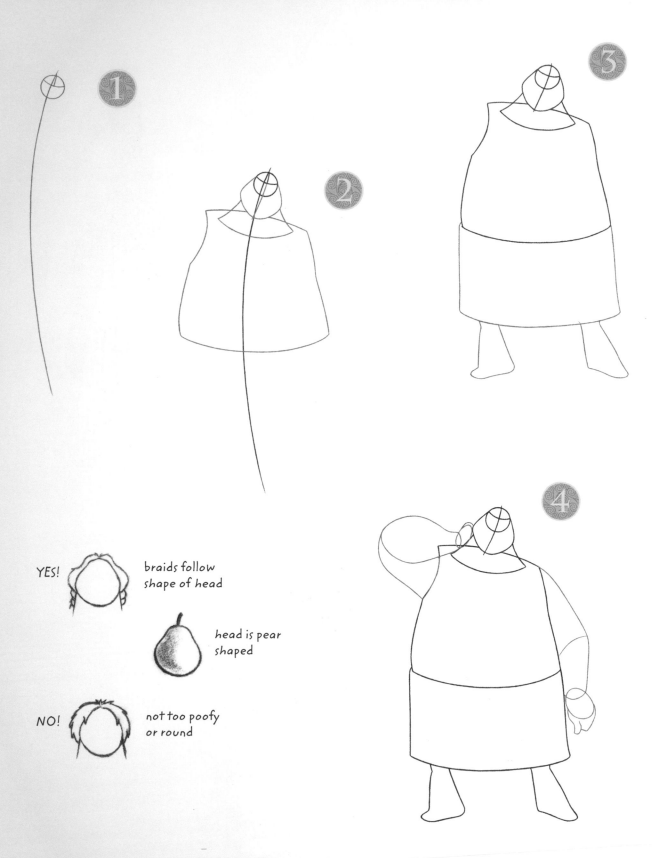

YES! braids follow
shape of head

head is pear
shaped

NO! not too poofy
or round

⑤

⑥

⑦

Young
MacGuffin

Lord
MacGuffin

THE CASTLE

The castle in the Scottish Highlands is home to Fergus; Elinor; Merida; and the triplets, Harris, Hubert, and Hamish. The Highland games take place here, where Merida shocks the whole kingdom.

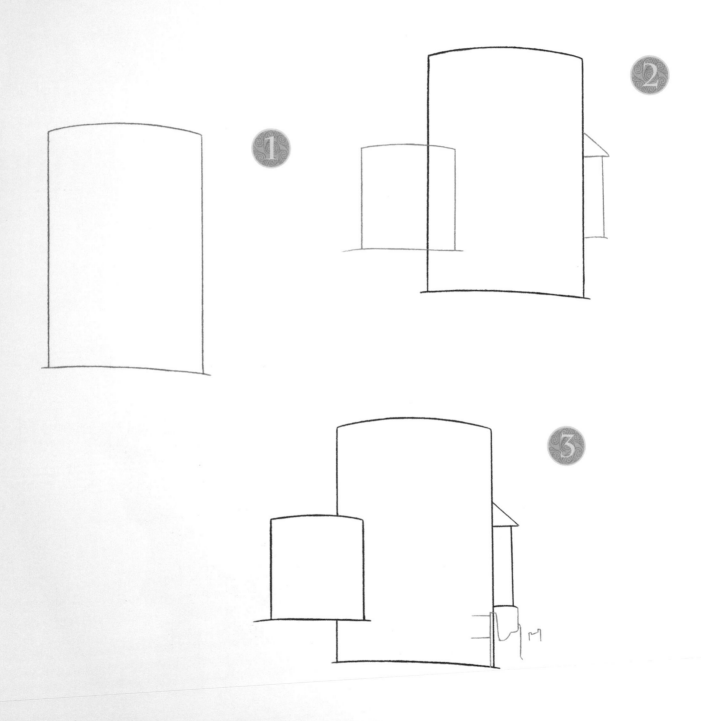

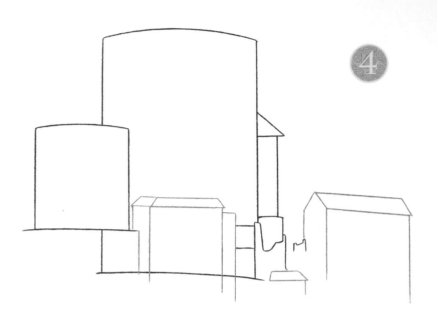

THE END

Now that you've learned the secrets to drawing the characters from *Brave*, try creating scenes from the movie or original scenes of your very own. You can draw Merida shooting her bow in a field or riding her horse through the forest, the triplets running through the hallways or causing mischief in the kingdom, or Fergus and Elinor laughing together. With the skills you've learned, the possibilities are endless! To be the maker of your own story, just like Merida, all you need is a piece of paper, a pencil, and your imagination!